TONES OF TRANSITION

Rebirth Through Language

FRANKLYN JAMES

Tones of Transition: Rebirth Through Language

Paperback ISBN: 979-8-9853434-4-1
E-Book ISBN: 979-8-9853434-5-8

TONES OF

TRANSITION

Contents

Hi friends,

As we pursue our dreams and desires, the language we use can get us stuck. I give you this piece of work hoping we can journey together into a new way of thinking and being.

Introduction

Tones of Transition is a conversation with myself into which I am inviting you. In this conversation, you will find the hindsight and the hidden wisdom I use to effectively process my thoughts. The ponderings are designed to expose negative and self-defeating thoughts, and to enter your own process of replacing them with constructive, life-building points of view.

Since our inward reflection directly influences the way our unconscious mind processes our wants and desires, this is a great resource to have.

Personal Statement

"The heights by great men reached and kept were not attained by sudden flight, but they, while their companions slept, were toiling upward in the night."
— *Henry Wadsworth Longfellow*

To reach the height of greatness, I must recognize the laws that are cognizant to my overall growth. These laws include the following:

The Law of Sacrifice: This means I must give up something good in the present to achieve something better in the future. This will be balanced by the Law of Reciprocity, in which I will get back what I give.

The Law of Consciousness: This means whatever I perceive or believe to be true will be true, even if it is in my life only.

Fear is a mirror that reflects my innermost thoughts and feelings. Fear must be dealt with for me to grow.

Love is the law that will allow me to help others realize their God-given potential.

I must keep moving onward, strive for perfection, and let integrity rule my life.

To fulfil these laws and insights, I must be conscious of my meditation, which will reveal my destiny.

Chapter **One**

The Lingua Lives:
Life in the Sounds of Your Mouth

Tones of Transition is a journey. It is a journey which began not with the idea of writing a book, but as a path to re-examining painful experiences, organizing my thoughts, and seeking healing through journaling my thoughts—thoughts that took on new dimensions when I realized that language helps create who we are and who we will become. Since I withdrew the previous version of this book, *Pocketful of Life*, a few years ago, I've gained a better understanding of how people communicate using the shared language of context in which everyone understands the nuances.

This often includes shared history, contemporary events, and social norms. We communicate these contextual events by using a symbolic communication system learned from the moment we are aware of sounds, sights, or feelings. Oftentimes, the meaning given to these symbols help us understand and communicate our ideas, thoughts, and emotions.

Not all communication is linguistic and not all language is verbal. However, since it is with language that we express the interpretation our thoughts and feelings, we need to pay attention to its usage.

Communication is the exchange of thoughts, feelings, or information by way of speech, signals, writing, or behaviour. For communication to be clear and free from misinterpretation, there must be a sender, there must be a medium of message—speaking, writing, signaling, or miming— and there must be feedback that the message was heard and understood.

In communication, we must always be aware that communication is either effective or ineffective. It is ineffective when a message is sent but is not received. Secondly, a message received but not understood is ineffective communication. A message sent, received, and understood is effective communication. Likewise, when there is a message sent and received, and a clarification is sought, there is effective communication.

In this collection, the term "language" refers to the meanings given to the thoughts, speech, emotions, and expressions of others. It also describes the things you keep saying to yourself based on your interpretation of life's circumstances, situations, and relationships. Considering this usage of language, learning from experiences, and developing a new mindset will help us construct sentences and phrases that allow us to move away from our negative, cyclical thinking.

Over time, I have learned it is often wise to change our speech when what we know is no longer helping us. Language forms our being; it shapes us and, in return, is shaped by us. It is the medium through which we learn new things and increase our awareness. Nevertheless, language can become a barrier, detrimental to our personal development, interactions, and goals.

Each word we use is filled with numerous personal meanings. The right words spoken in the right manner can bring us love, harmony, and wealth. For example, Marah has had a devastating life experience—she has recently lost a loved one in an accident and was herself in a life-changing accident.

Using words such as, "I am here if you need me" or "If there's anything I can do, let me know when you are ready," can give Marah the assurance that she doesn't have to talk about the issue in that moment, and that you will be there or available if she needs you during that difficult time.

On the other hand, our concern for Marah, coupled with anxiety, can cause us to try consoling her with words such as, "Everything will be fine" or "It's the god's will." In her state of grief and pain, Marah may not be ready to hear such words, whether or not the words are true or possible. Most often, these words inflict further pain on the person. In both examples, the importance of being mindful with our words cannot be stressed enough.

Life can be defined as the quality of existence in which an individual processes, acts, and evolves through an evolutionary process. That is, an individual is born, goes through developmental cycles, shares in the lived experiences of others, feels and expresses various emotions and thoughts, and eventually dies.

A person does not only exist for existence's sake. Each person has his or her purpose in life, or a purpose for living. This motivation or reason to get up each day guides their decisions, determines their life's goals, affects their behaviour, and offers some sense of direction. Generally, activities give meaning to existence, causing someone to be happy and seek to share this lifestyle.

People of all ages, and throughout the ages, have engaged in activities that lead to a life of meaning and promote happiness. They also seek to preserve life and a purpose for living. Yet, throughout history, we read about people who used their words to take life from others. One incomparable period was the Holocaust in the 1930s and '40s, in which fearful and hateful language was used to annihilate a group of people from existence.

There is similar rhetoric being used today that was used in the Holocaust to eliminate groups of people from various nations and to boost nationalism. This includes similar anti-Semitic rhetoric, rhetoric of making a nation "great again," rhetoric that immigrants from certain countries are threats to countries to which they are trying to migrate, and rhetoric using war language to defend nationalism and the expansion of power.

We have used the power of words to persuade others to act tyrannically or compassionately, and to shape the course of language itself.

Until we change the way we think, we will become or continue being verbal assassins in our personal and social worlds, using our words like guns and swords to shoot down and pierce the souls of others. We become unwitting slayers because we do not pay attention to the things we are saying to ourselves and to others. This careless cycle of verbal abuse and verbal assassination can only be changed by modifying the way we think and speak.

The way we communicate is very important and necessary for personal well-being and interpersonal relationships. The language used by partners, relatives, or a small community and the language used by a country are two different aspects of the same language. The first is more private, while the other is public. An increased awareness of each society and its subcultures having their own languages that intersect to varying degrees will assist us to be more responsible in our own expressions.

Acquiring new language or a new way of speaking to ourselves and others will require that we pay keen attention to its acquisition. Attention must be given also to the acquisition of new languages, since we acquire new languages throughout our lives as we interact with diverse cultures.

Learning languages that give life cannot be left to fate—or fate will be fateful. That is, if we believe that being in poor relationships or unsatisfactory jobs are inevitable, we will not think of other possibilities. We believe it is fated. In these situations, we will not seek to examine our thoughts and language since we have not made the connection between what we think, say, and do, and our current situation. In this way, fate will faithfully provide us poor relationships or jobs.

To escape this vicious cycle, you need to become intentional in that which you think about. This process involves apprehending a thought that has the potential to do harm, reflecting on the thought, seeking alternative ways of thinking, and then using the alternative thoughts to inform your speech and actions.

Acquiring or blocking new language has the potential to produce emotional, social, and behavioural practices that are unhealthy for an individual. For example, you meet a person whose thoughts and experiences are different from yours. After spending time with this person, you begin to apply the language they use in your circumstances, situations, and relationships. Soon, your life and relationships begin to fall apart. This happens because the self-talk of another person or group is not always compatible with our experiences.

It is crucial we remain conscious of the fact that we experience circumstances, situations, and relationships through language. Over the years, I've realized the language I spoke caused much of the pain and trauma in my life to be more difficult than it should have been. I kept hurting myself and falling into the same situations repeatedly. This was not because I wasn't intelligent; it was because the language I spoke was limited and negative. My self-talk was not consistent with my goals and desires.

Fait accompli refers to an action which is completed before those affected by it can change it. This same principle can be applied to the things we think and speak. In most instances, it's after we say something that we regret it. Saying the right thing or speaking positively begins by preparing yourself to overcome negative self-talk, renewing your mindsets, and transforming your ways of communicating with others. This task will require discipline and patience. The caterpillar/butterfly analogy illustrates this beautifully.

> A caterpillar's life begins as the egg of a butterfly laid on the underside of a leaf. After the caterpillar hatches from the egg, it eats the leaves. During this period, it experiences tremendous growth. The caterpillar sheds its skin, becoming larger and stronger. At the right time, the caterpillar spins a cocoon, then enters it.

It is during this process that a change of the form and nature of the caterpillar occurs. It becomes a completely different thing: a beautiful butterfly. This illustration effectively demonstrates the process through which we can renew our minds. It begins with our self-talk.

Ideally, the ability to use hindsight and foresight creates the awesome life we want. However, this will only happen as we become conscious of how, when, and where we are, and to whom we are saying what. Not being aware of these things can hinder you in maintaining a happy life. A critical part of a happy life is having authentic relationships. It is why in building relationships, we look forward to seeing them being satisfying and enduring.

When expectations are not expressed or poorly communicated in a relationship, it causes serious problems.

Expecting a positive response from a partner or prospective partner is a part of socialization in any cultural context, and as such, expectations must be communicated effectively and clearly. Never assume your partner, relatives, or friends know what you expect of them. This attitude is immature and will frustrate you each time someone in the relationship does not act in the way you expected.

When examining our thoughts and words, forgiveness is very important. Not only does forgiveness clear the conscience and free our minds, but it also helps us maintain personal integrity, wholeness with ourselves. Forgiveness does not mean all things are completely restored or that you will not feel angry about an offense committed against you. The key idea is to forgive the person for the action; it is the action itself that has offended you. In our process of change and creating new ways of expressing ourselves, we must forgive self and others and move on. Why?

Because it is common for us as individuals or groups to look at our problems and think that if our past had been different, our circumstances, situations, and relationships today would be different. However, this type of thinking is self-defeating and unprofitable because our physiological functioning and time move only forward. Let us forgive so we create the atmosphere to produce life-giving words.

Each statement in *Tones of Transition* reveals how the things we say mirror and affect important aspects of our lives. The right word or phrase can stimulate our minds and open our awareness to exploring our worlds. Becoming conscious of your thoughts, emotions, and actions will help you to avoid being in a situation in which you feel you are living in a stranger's body and don't know what it will do.

I know you may find some of the statements negative and contradictory. However, each thought conveys life and must be examined. It is only after analyzing a thought that we can know whether to change it. It is my hope your awareness will increase and you experience a rebirth from the ponderings in this book.

Chapter **Two**

Emerge and Evolve:
Hello from the Inside

You may often hear versions of the quotes, "From the abundance of the heart the mouth speaks," and "It is what comes out of a person that defiles." Both these quotes can be found in many sacred and philosophical works in one form or another. These truisms are often as true as truisms can get. When we express what we are thinking and feeling or our goals and desires, we affect and are affected by the recipients of those emotions and goals in one way or another. This happens instinctively and on a subconscious level, through words, thoughts, feelings, and body language. In fact, most individuals will agree it is preferable to be around positive people while avoiding negative people. This is because both positive and negative ways of thinking are contagious.

People are more willing to help us if we are positive, and they are likely to avoid anyone who displays negative behaviour and attitudes. Negative thoughts, words, and attitude create negative and unhappy feelings, moods, and behaviour.

Overcoming negative mindsets for a transformed and authentic life requires discipline and patience. The analogy of a butterfly illustrates this effectively.

This transformation of the caterpillar into a butterfly, used in Chapter One, can be used to explain liberation from exilic experience in our lives and the personal freedom achieved when a person refines his or her character traits. New thought can be seen as a paradigm shift from the norm. It is often revolutionary and worth celebrating.

A positive attitude can help us experience life experiences in a temperate and fulfilling way. Even our health can be affected in a constructive way. We tend to walk more purposefully and speak with confidence with a positive attitude. In short, our body language shows the way we feel.

> Positive thinking is a mental and emotional attitude that focuses on the bright side of life and the expectations of positive results. A person with positive thinking anticipates happiness, health, and success, and believes that he or she can overcome any obstacle and difficulty.

Steps to Thinking Positively

Positive thinking cannot be forced. Neither can positive ways of being. In many instances, we are so emotionally invested in a person, situation, or circumstance that we can't just think our way out. On the other hand, negative thinking is generally harmful to the self and others. As a result, cultivating the mindset to think anew is important.

Some basic steps we can take in changing our thoughts include:

- Being aware that some inner or soul work is required. Since attitude and thoughts were developed over time, they will not change overnight.
- Smiling and laughing more. Smiling makes you more attractive and approachable. This will help gain new relationships and improve self-confidence. What's more, endorphins are released when you smile and will make you feel less stressed and happier.
- Not worrying about what other people say or think about you, especially if they discover that you are trying to change the way you think. However, you can ask those who genuinely want to see you thrive what they think of you.
- Using your imagination to visualize favorable and beneficial situations. Make your gut feeling a close friend.
- Using positive words in your self-talk, and when talking with others. This is the power of conscious positive expressions.

> Not forcing positive or negative thoughts to remain or to go away. Sometimes all we need to do is to examine thoughts in their entirety. This will require living a meditative lifestyle. Finding a conclusion to a situation is helpful; so too is realizing there won't be an answer to every situation.

- Being prepared to move on without closure, and being patient. Closure doesn't always come immediately, if at all.

Once a negative thought enters your mind, you have to be aware of it and endeavor to replace it with a constructive one. Persistence will eventually teach and train your mind to think positively and pragmatically without ignoring negative thoughts.

If you are like me, you may want to give up on the task to work on your thoughts and words when you are facing conflicts and resistance within yourself. Do not yield to this temptation. Keep anticipating the beneficial, favourable, and happy outcomes. It doesn't matter what your circumstances are now—never stop thinking positively.

If you persevere, you will transform both the way you think speak and the way you ultimately behave. It will take some time for the changes to take place, but eventually they will through perseverance. Reciting words of affirmation and visualizing positive outcomes is an integral part of the process. After reciting affirming words and visualizing the outcomes we desire, the outcomes become easier to attain.

In addition to the steps listed above, we need to know ourselves. This involves three things: improving your self-esteem, creating flexible boundaries, and nurturing development.

Improve Your Self-Esteem

Sharing what we feel and need takes courage. Without a healthy self-esteem, we will take things too personally. This often leads to feelings of shame and guilt. In this state, our self-defense mechanism kicks in and threatens our emotional safety and, in turn, our self-esteem. Building healthy self-esteem includes becoming vulnerable. This is necessary, as it also builds confidence.

Create Flexible Boundaries

Healthy self-esteem and a deeper connection to our authentic self help us define our boundaries. We become confident in our capabilities—what we can endure and what we cannot. Flexible boundaries also enable us to discern when, where, how, and with whom we can be vulnerable. These boundaries allow us to be aware of our differences with others, and of our uniqueness.

Flexible boundaries allow us to be our best selves in the company of family, peers, and colleagues. If we are without boundaries, we will attract circumstances, situations, and relations that will work against our goal of changing our thoughts and conversations. Knowing this well brings us a new way of thinking, a new way of life.

Nurture Your Development

We cannot control another person's reaction or behaviour. However, we can nurture and sustain ourselves based on healthy moral and spiritual practices. This increases our autonomy, interdependence, and self-sustenance.

Nurturing your development also includes creating time and space for learning. This involves learning about *you* and allotting time to improve yourself spiritually, emotionally, socially, financially, and academically. The level of our success hinges on supporting others who are trying to achieve the same goals as us. It aids in nurturing ourselves.

Therefore, you can see the importance of nurturing a new way of life to fit your new way of thinking. Having supportive relationships and the ability to comfort each another makes us less dependent-minded.

My Ponderings

Become the artist who designs your own life. While others look at life's straight lines—their height, depth, and width—bend the lines with your imagination, turning greys and white into shades of blue and yellow and a tint of controversy.

We exist in more than one world; our personal world and the universal community share with all creation.

The results of humanity's fallen state can be traced throughout history and are demonstrated by the malady and misery we face today.

You need to question the popularity of a taught belief system to determine whether it meets God's expectations for you.

**"Spring is the season when poets'
pens ponder. They ponder romance
and the promise of new life."**

Spirituality has two birthing places: a divine source
and the search within to find oneself. Rarely do
we pursue both; we seek one above the other.

**"To be spiritual is to be sexual; to
be sexual is to be human; and
to be human is to be alive."**

Like an eagle free from the trap of its captives, there
should be no fear of soaring to new heights.

Life's complexities give meaning to our
existence, not an uncomplex way of being.

When we learn to escape the traps and limitations of one's context, there is now no fear left of the unknown.

"Life is the only gift to which a price tag must not be attached."

The absence of love is the presence of hell.

In this generation, sin is called anything except sin.

Cry as we may that there is no God;
we only confirm that God is.

In attaining a new paradigm, we must remember that the desire and necessity to be different are conceived and birthed out of our challenges.

In acquiring a new language, we need to know what to retain and what to reject.

"I love the person I've become because I fought to become him."

In the vastness of human experiences, whether in ease or dilemmas, there is often space for the greater display of the goodness of God! Whatever you face, be it yesterday, today, or tomorrow, I am persuaded that God can bring you out gloriously and provide answers to any doubt that may assail you.

"Fear of the otherness is the fear of life."

Whatever happens to other seeds does not affect a specific seed. Each seed sticks to its own task.

Self-esteem provides a mindset that prepares an individual to respond according to expectations of success, failures, and personal strength.

Healthy expectations towards self when encountering physical and emotional pain and weaknesses are essential for your development.

"Talking about your dream creates a network of people who will work with you and support your dream."

Living your life by someone else's expectations will cost you more than you are willing to give.

Often, we burn our souls chasing after our hearts' desires. Only through the transformation of our total being can we turn the ash into gold.

Preoccupation with your personal sphere of influence and its troublesome relations ought to be your primary concern.

The challenges of life do not prevent us from living enriching lives; they teach us how to strive for success.

Knowing who you are, what you need, and the reason you need it will empower you to make your dreams a reality consciously and actively.

"Most of our life is spent in an
unconscious state, unaware
of what we are choosing in the
way of thoughts, speech, and
actions until we experience
the consequences of them."

When you encounter unplanned obstacles, persistence
will allow you to maintain your course and see
obstacles not as problems but opportunities.

Success does not occur in a vacuum; we need people
in our lives to assist us in realizing our full potential.

When changing our belief system, we need to discard
the negatives and remove any doubts and beliefs that are
inconsistent with our desired goal swiftly and firmly.

"When your self-esteem is affected by emotions, the way you interact with the environment, or your perception of what others think of you, you have a fundamental problem. Find out what it is."

Our vision of what we want to do will guide us; hence, it is necessary for us to see this vision as clearly as possible.

Accept your present status, change your attitude, and you will possess your dream.

A healthy dose of self-pride will allow you to accomplish unimaginable success.

Discipline is the key to success in creating your new life. It will teach you that life is not a smooth journey; there will be rough spots.

"A person was not created to be alone; we were created to love and support each other. This is part of a divine plan."

How I see myself will influence my behavior; if I label myself as a social animal, I will behave like an animal.

Amid life's chaos, people are beginning to understand the need for authentic companionship.

Silence will cultivate comfort and peace in your life.

"A heart that thirsts for romantic love cannot be quenched by any other passion, position, or property."

Without love, I am a roving fool, relentlessly seeking fame and fortune.

We must discard anything in our lives that threatens our quest for freedom, success, and growth.

Being too selective and arrogant can reduce one's chances of finding a compatible partner.

One of the greatest sources of satisfaction comes from the knowledge that other people think well of us.

**"Being authentic includes who
I am and who you say I am, as
long as it agrees with who
my Creator says I am."**

Although our desires may be instinctual, our
motivation to attain them is based solely on our
impulses, which are determined and shaped by
societal norms and our preferences and wants.

Loneliness will only be cured by a
voluntary desire to reclaim your life.

**"We must not focus on the mountain
of trials, despairs, and difficulties,
or we will miss the victory."**

We must cultivate meaningful relationships and wait for a bountiful harvest of friendship and love.

You are not the same person who made mistakes yesterday. When you look in the mirror today, you see someone who has grown, shaped by those experiences, yet is still unique and gifted.

Instead of denouncing the evil of sin, we excuse it, deny it, defend it, or try to understand it.

"A person's spirituality is what allows that person to experience the otherness of a Creator, Divine Being, Nature, or Cosmos."

We are all unique, with different traits, weaknesses, and strengths, and each one of us has been created to love and be loved.

To escape a hopeless cycle, separate
your wants from your needs.

When we have a clear idea of where we are going and
the confidence that we have the right idea, positive
outcomes are the consequences of our actions.

Hate suffocates the imagination,
where creativity unfolds.

**"Only in dreams do I
escape your tyranny."**

Chapter **Three**

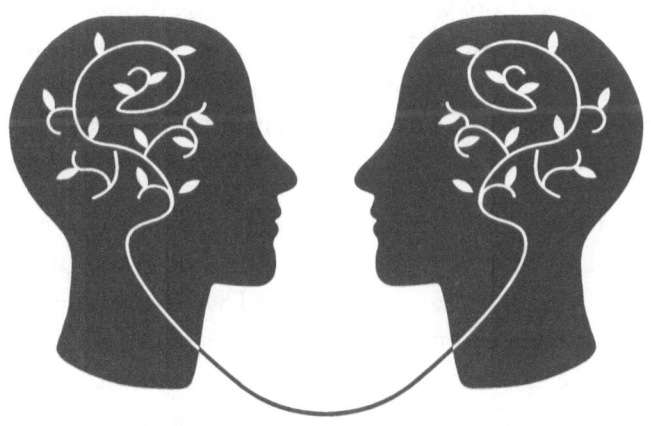

Meeting Myself:
Thoughts from the Deep

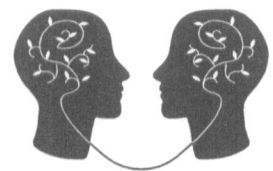

S peaking life into others or to the self requires proper self-management. As such, we must consciously choose how we live our lives. This thought itself is a paradox. How can I be asked to consciously choose to live when I am awake, alive, and functioning? This is an interesting dilemma because oftentimes we are awake, yet we are not conscious of the things we are saying and doing.

These things have become so normal, we do not realize them. In other words, we are not conscious of many of the things we say and do until we experience their negative consequences. On the other hand, we may say and do certain things, but because the consequences in the here and now are pleasurable to us, we cannot see the negative impact it is having on others and the influence on our future.

Explicitly saying what we think and feel are not the only ways we reveal in words what thoughts and feelings we are having. Therefore, it is critical to distinguish between verbal expressions of our thoughts and feelings from nonverbal expressions.

In contemporary worlds, freedom of expression is the mantra. Regrettably, this freedom to express oneself has been abused to the point where it intrudes on the rights of others. This creates a situation in which we must be conscious of how, when, and where we are at all times, and to whom we are expressing what. While freedom of expression is a fundamental human right, it must be wielded with responsibility. Not being aware of these things can hinder you in attaining your goals.

It is often said that an unbridled tongue is as dangerous as a snake. I can remember several instances in which unconscious expressions by a quick tongue have driven individuals into trouble. This situation is similar to that of a furious horse who needs a bridle to restrain its fierceness and energy. This can be a guide for us, since the tongue of a person needs restraint to keep it in from inflicting hurtful words on the self and others.

The individual who desires and seeks to enjoy quiet and peaceful living must guard over his or her mouth and refrain from scandalous and divisive conversations. Avoiding unpleasant conversation, foolish talk, and irrelevant jesting are vital to the process of becoming conscious of our expressions. Indeed, a person's life truly can be measured by the words they speak. It should be no surprise, then, that some of the contemporary problematic situations we encounter are the consequence of words spoken in the past.

Developing a healthy vocabulary for feelings such as guilt, fear, shame, anger, happiness, and joy will help us to be understood and be better communicators, as well as get us what we need. Expressing ourselves in rage is oftentimes a defense for shame and guilt. This way of being will cause damage to our relationships with others and push them away. This is usually the opposite of what we really want. Likewise, if we believe we should be all-sufficient or too self-sufficient, we might not meet our need for meaningful support and closeness to others. This may lead to us feeling lonely and resentful.

In our quest to express those thoughts that are deep within or to be conscious of our expressions, there are three things to bear in mind.

Honor Your Feelings and Needs

We must not only acknowledge but honor our feelings and needs if we are going to reveal them to others. We must also become aware of the shame and guilt that are concealed and the contempt we hold against our feelings and needs. If you need the help of a skilled therapist to help you in accepting your needs without self-judgment, you should seek one.

Bear in mind: families and close friends or a spiritual guide, clergyperson, imam, or other can be of great help. Do not forget the importance a journal or diary to use as an avenue to vent your true feelings so you can examine them later.

Be Assertive, Not Pushy or Aggressive

There are constructive and destructive ways to communicate our vulnerability. Many of us lack proper role models, both in our families and in society, who exemplify healthy and proper assertion of self. Therefore, developing an assertiveness skill is very important, not only because it builds self-esteem, but because it also enables us to communicate in effective ways that promote deeper connection with others.

This way of being is helpful when we need to ask for feedback about something negative or something that is bothering us. It may include feelings about someone we dislike or something we don't want. Additionally, when we set limits and know when to say yes or no whenever necessary, we might be able to save ourselves from more awkward situations which may come later.

Be Gracious

> Being gracious includes a person's effort not to hurt others with careless words and tactless deeds. They try to be discretionary in their words and actions.

For example, a gracious person will apologize to you even when they are right, before there is a misunderstanding. If you are a person of faith in a divine Being, you will develop a disposition to cooperate with this Being and create a more peaceful and loving world.

Being gracious includes going beyond and above what is expected for your well-being and that of others. We must also bear this in mind: when we interact with others in any situation, good or bad, our body language projects to some degree the consciousness of our thoughts. To put it more explicitly, body language reflects what goes on in our mind. This is a telling aspect of our inner thoughts and feelings.

My Ponderings

Careful orchestration of words is like completing
a masterpiece. Each note is arranged to achieve
connectivity, harmony, and success.

Temptations stimulate or appeal to our desires.

Without the aid of a rational mind, desires and
pleasures will create chaos in our lives.

To be effective, temptation must remind us
of the pleasure we once enjoyed or introduce
us to a new stimulus through our desires.

When a person is rejected, it is like a million
daggers piercing the soul, giving birth to bitterness
and temporary leave of their sensibility.

It is not that we err as human beings; it is that
we are expected to err. This expectation to
err defeats our will to attain the ideal life.

"It is a distressing reality to acknowledge that sins are mistakes, but not all mistakes are sins."

It is sensible for us to know where innocence and ignorance end and responsibility and guilt begin.

Despite the influences that inform our irrational decisions, the choice is always present to make rational ones.

A moment in tears can give birth to a new life. This allows for the transformation of our whole being. It is a time of refreshing.

Accepting the otherness of life gives our thoughts a transcendent dimension, allowing us to transcend our immediate circumstances in space and time.

"Life is like a whirlwind, and I am
in the center. I let in what might,
cannot see what ought, and
worry about what should have."

The jester says, "If I am only responsible for what
I know, wouldn't it benefit me to avoid learning to
be responsible for my life's choices? In this way, I
cannot be held responsible for my failures."

Any attempt to alter our natural state is
a revelation of our inauthenticity.

When you are unsure of yourself or expect to fail
at a task, you are inclined to stop trying, give up,
and miss an opportunity to gain experience.

"Ownership is empowering; it drives us to acquire the skills we need when we don't yet possess them."

Your success depends on your judgment of worthiness expressed by the values and attitudes you hold for yourself.

A healthy dose of pride will allow you to accomplish remarkable things.

I thought I was free, but it was only a dream.

Trying to change without knowing who you are is impossible.

If a person believes he or she is going to fail, they will find a way to fail.

If you do not accept yourself for who you truly are, you are not going to accept anyone for who they truly are.

"The source of your pain: do you know it?"

Rejection can shatter our perceptions like glass, sending shards of shock and shivers in us.

The first step in increasing your self-esteem is to transform your thought process.

Our success will remain static if we follow the concept of "should," an obligation imposed by outside influences.

"Since humanity has a past, we often make the mistake of looking at our problems and saying if our past had been different, our circumstances, situations, and relationships would be different today, preventing us from fully embracing the present and shaping a better future."

You exist for a purpose. When you act outside of that purpose, you are an inauthentic person.

To move forward with your vision, you need to identify the challenges and opportunities in your life. Otherwise, you will be like a plane in the clouds without a compass, soaring aimlessly.

Behind many smiles lies a pain the
world will never understand.

I planned to sit here just a little while and
work on attaining my dreams. I never knew I
would become dry bones—empty, visionless,
and apathetic—while still sitting here.

"Judging ourselves unfavorably, hoping it will motivate us to change, only works in the short term."

Negative self-talk can make us feel bad about
ourselves and deplete our energy by working
against the change we want to accomplish.

Allowing your unidentified thought processes
to determine your feelings and actions will
keep you in your own internal dramas.

Loneliness points to a fact: if our need for
social relationships is not met, we can fall
apart physically, mentally, and spiritually.

We fail to trust others when we lose trust in ourselves.
How can we relate to others if our hearts are closed?

Intimacy requires being aware of one's self-
identity, including one's innermost thoughts,
feelings, and expectations, in order to
share oneself genuinely with another.

With loneliness come wasted opportunities and lost
possibilities for friendships and relationships.

**"I roamed the length and breadth
of the Earth to escape you. Yet my
love for you remains with me."**

Loneliness is not a mystery and may require in-depth counseling and guidance to navigate.

Relationships with other human beings are important in developing our human capabilities and being one with each other and the Creator.

Commitment is the will to maintain the bond in a relationship that keeps partners together.

Relationships are investments. The more you invest, the greater your return.

One outcome of fear is the inability to express yourself because of what you perceive others might think of you.

The most hurtful yet normal feeling to experience is loneliness.

Self-preservation causes people to enter
relationships with distrust, reservation,
and fear of being rejected and hurt.

Bemoaning the insecurity of seeking happiness
through relationships can leave one feeling
so void that it borders on coldness.

**"Four things are sought after in
this world: love, fame, wealth,
and power. Yet, rarely do these
share each other's company."**

Emptiness can stem from a need that one is
not yet conscious of or result from an awakened
consciousness of inconsistencies in one's life.

Growth in a relationship is realized when expectations are manageable, and the differences between interests are balanced.

Being there is the best gift you can give someone worried they may live out their lives without someone to share intimate moments and camaraderie—a friend.

Faithlessness and sarcasm say, "People are so fickle these days; just listen, smile, and do what you were going to do anyway."

There is no greater tragedy than that moment when you realize you are in love, but it cannot be shown or told to anyone.

"If I alter who I am to become who I am, what truth does that reveal, and what does it say about who I am?"

Apathy says, "I am going to die with a crush
on you and not be able to nurture it into
the greatest love story of all time."

Only in the arms of my beloved will the tempest
of this world's splendors be tempered.

A person will always have time to be alone,
either by circumstance or choice.

Fearing whether a person will like you
can be disastrous in building bonds.

To be victorious in weakness, we must cultivate the
type of friendships in which accountability occurs
naturally; this requires an investment of time.

A sad reality is that people are entering relationships with barriers protecting themselves from intimacy with others and their feelings.

No matter how much I gained, my heart remains troubled without someone to dote on with love.

"In the stillness of our souls, the loudest truths are spoken."

Chapter **Four**

Molded by Our Words:
When the Reflection in the
Mirror Starts Speaking

I **F** you have read this far in this book, you have already realized how much we are shaped by our words. In addition, we are shaping the way people react and the way the universe reacts and responds to us. Therefore, we must be mindful when we are having conversation with others because we are both sending and receiving two messages. The first message is the conscious one we are aware of, the one we articulate. That is why the quote "Be conscious of our meditation" is so important.

In many of our conversations, we try to withhold our true feelings and thoughts. Regrettably, they can still manifest themselves in our body language and in our aura. This is a second way of communicating. This aura, or idiosyncratic quality, is our unique marker or characteristic as a person. Someone who is authentic and in tune with their spiritual and emotional self can discern our thoughts and feelings.

If we are not conscious that is dual dialogue is taking place, we will have either of two consequences. The less dramatic consequence is we make attaining our goals and the authentic relationships more difficult. On the other extreme, we will never attain the goals and relationships we desire. When building relationships, we look forward to seeing them being satisfying and enduring, but we must make sure the things we want to say are the things we are saying, consciously and unconsciously.

When we are not conscious of our expressions, they will deflect from others what we are expressing. That is, people are going to give back to us what they receive from us. It's like talking in an echo chamber while looking at yourself in a mirror. Therefore, communicate your intentions and expectations clearly. When communication is not clear in a relationship or when intentions and expectations are not realized, they cause serious problems.

Expecting a positive response from a partner or prospective partner is a part of socialization in any cultural context, and as such, expectations must be communicated effectively and clearly. Lack of authenticity can distort our communication. This, in turn, damages relationships as we seek to control, patronize, criticize, blame, deny, withdraw, attack, or make empty promises to keep a relationship, reassuring ourselves we're okay even when we don't believe it.

In relationships, never assume your partner, relatives, or friends know what you expect of them. Some people are fond of giving the silent treatment whenever a loved one offends them.

> There is no need for grudges if you are not bold enough to express what is damaging your relationship with others.

This attitude is immature and will frustrate you each time someone in the relationship does not act according to your expectation. Clear and effective communication and the right mindset are important in relationships.

As we get to know our partners better in a relationship, it is common to discover things we dislike. Our feelings will get deeply hurt, our needs will conflict, and we will have varied disagreements. To try to make the relationship last, we start keeping things to ourselves, withdrawing, and sometimes trying to change our partner into the person we think they ought to be. As time goes by, the risk of being vulnerable and honest with each other becomes increasingly difficult. This fail-prone approach to relationship happens when we try to control the people we are involved with, as well as trying to control the relationship itself.

In the situation described, words of love are spoken but passion and intimacy are missing. One or both partners yearn for connection but feel empty and lonely due to their fear of rejection and loss. We keep enduring, and when the relationship ends, we are deeply hurt.

This is usually the point in our relationship where emotional intelligence in handling such situations comes in. Books, workshops, and discussions on social intelligence and emotional intelligence are available to help us become more competent in these areas of our lives. I encourage you invest in one of these. This education makes it possible for individuals to not only appreciate the task of monitoring and naming their feelings and emotions, but also to learn to guide their thoughts and actions, as well as how to express them.

The way we express our hurt, dreams, aspirations, and disappointments matters a lot. For example, if I sense a readiness for empathizing and trying to understand my partner's view, I find they are usually willing to talk, apologize, and turn a new leaf. Unfortunately, ego sometimes gets in the way for those who are not emotionally sensitive whenever there is a conflict, and situations normally get worse.

Reflection on our relationships and the words we use are essential to the authentic expression of our feelings towards others. Yet sometimes we find ourselves struggling with expressing who we are and what we need. It will help us in our interpersonal relationships to be self-aware, focus on being gracious, and listen to our gut feelings.

My Ponderings

You cannot become authentic outside
the parameters of the Creator.

Any effort by ourselves to be authentic is futile.

"To be authentic, we must be aware of who we are and what we were created for."

Authenticity stems from a divine imperative
and not from any created source.

A tyrant is born when genuine concern
for justice gives way to self-interest.

Nature or the impulse of nature is unable to produce
an authentic being. The divine spark is needed.

Without Yahweh, all humanity is like an empty shell.

"There are only setbacks when hurdles become deterrents."

Authenticity can only be achieved by connecting with the divine.

It is only when the supernatural governs the natural that authenticity is born.

Love has the power of the dew of the morning: caressing all that nature produces and washing the dross from the soul.

"A seed contains life. Yet it does nothing until planted at the appointed time in the appropriate place."

I have limited power over the things in the world but unlimited power over the things in my personal world.

God always remains God alone, and humanity always remains a creature dependent upon God.

"Once we discard our old biases and our bipolar and linear ways of thinking, we will invoke the aid of the highest sources of knowledge to assist us in conceiving a new way of experiencing the manifested existence of the divine, the self, and others."

Whatsoever problems are perceived with religion will be found in your personal philosophy.

The greater the obstacles in your life, the greater
the success and the more glorious the reward.

A person going through a transformation is like water.
After it has been transformed into ice or gas, it will
always maintain its originality, but its quality is forever
changed, and it reacts and behaves differently to stimuli.

Diversity in creation is not by blind
chance; it results from the purpose of an
unchangeable and unmovable force.

"Without accepting the otherness of others, our thoughts will favor the death of others."

What concern should I have with the
general world when I cannot master the
complexities of my personal landscapes?

"Self-acceptance involves being happy with yourself as you are now. It is an agreement with yourself to love and appreciate you."

The prudent person does not allow another person's reaction or opinion to change their value and worth.

"It is essential to accept each other's personal backgrounds, thoughts, and experiences. Yet, recognizing when change is necessary is equally important."

Our beliefs form the foundation of our attitude and behavior. Pay attention to them.

Experiencing depression can drive one insane.

The past does not affect your future; your
present choices and actions do.

When you begin to put your desires
into words, they become real.

When you are the owner, there is no other
course of action but to take ownership.

**"The opportunity to be a tyrant
is ever present in our quest to
maintain justice and create hope."**

Success is impossible without taking
ownership of your life, your choices, your
actions, and the resulting consequences.

Humanity cannot change its past. The most it can
do is build a new history from the present.

"If you do not take ownership for achieving your dreams, then circumstances, situations, and relationships will."

Do not use me as a target for your words. They hold the capacity to kill me emotionally, spiritually, and physically.

Acceptance will help both partners effectively cope with behaviors undermining a relationship while awaiting the expected change.

Lust is a deep desire to have someone or something for pleasure or gain. Lust has the potential of blossoming into love, which is selfless, with a deep desire not only to have someone but to connect and be with someone eternally.

"Writing rids the soul of pain."

People are created to form meaningful human relationships with each other. These must not be replaced with pets, professions, or hobbies.

Why is it that lovers wander the universe trying to escape love, only to discover the beloved may be absent, but their love remains in the heart?

Authentic relationships can be destroyed by a sense of inadequacy and feeling unworthy of intimacy because of not being accepted in the past.

"Immoral attitude, thoughts, or behavior is a secret friend; it is a friendship we learn to depend on emotionally when we feel insecure and alone."

Relationships are like houses. To avoid destroying our lives and the lives of others, we must begin our relationships with careful planning.

Effective communication is the steel and the cornerstone that will keep a relationship solid and able to survive life's rigors.

Patience will allow you to know others.

Weaknesses are not failures.

Intimacy is a basic ingredient in any meaningful relationship, the basis of friendship, and a foundations of love.

"Forming casual connections can be effortless, but building a lasting, meaningful relationship often requires time and intention."

Accepting that we are loved and accepted will free us to love and accept others.

Being real is not an excuse to be mean.

It is easy to be attracted to many people and share some degree of love with them, but a deeper connection will exist with one person.

"Lust is selfish and will wear out with no resentment, pain, or sense of loss. Love, on the other hand, leaves a feeling of loss and a deep yearning."

Irrespective of the wisdom of the wise or the folly of fools, the heart wants what the heart wants.

Cheating is a selfish hobby with little consideration for others.

The love that makes us authentic does not come from the natural world; it is transcendental.

"Romance can be full of heartaches and poetry; do not fall prey by trying to save those who are like jackals lurking among ruins instead of running from them."

About the Author

Franklyn James, originally from Jamaica and now residing in Canada, is an educator, pastoral counselor, and artist with a rich background in theology and education. His work centers on fostering holistic growth in others, embodying his belief in the transformative power of personal experiences and acquired knowledge.

An enthusiastic advocate for social justice and personal transformation, Franklyn's writing often explores these themes. As a critical thinker, he encourages questioning traditional and contemporary rhetoric, offering a fresh and insightful perspective on inclusivity and justice.

Franklyn's ability to inspire new ways of thinking is showcased in his other works, including *Shards of Longing*, a collection of dark poetry; *The Little Things We Take for Granted*, a delightful poetic journey into the simple joys of life for both children and adults; and *The Body in Narrative: A Writer's Guide to Character Reaction*, offering fresh insights into storytelling through the use of body language and physical expression.

If you enjoyed *Tones of Transition*, please consider leaving a review.